# PROPHETIC RAIN

### 21 days of prophetic prayers to shift your drought atmosphere

## TAMMY JAÉ

*I dedicate this book to the*
*One who picked me up, dusted me off,*
*and called me His own. You are the Author and*
*Finisher*
*of my Faith, my First Love, and my All in All.*
*I love You, because You first loved me.*
*Your daughter, Tammy*

*But blessed is the one who trusts in the Lord,*
*whose confidence is in him.*
*They will be like a tree planted by the water*
*that sends out its roots by the stream.*
*It does not fear when heat comes;*
*its leaves are always green.*
*It has no worries in a year of drought*
*and never fails to bear fruit.*

*-Jeremiah 17:7-8, NIV*

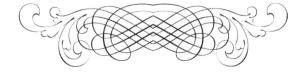

## Prophetic

*My doctrine shall drop as the rain, my speech shall distill as the dew,*

*as the small rain upon the tender herb,*

*and as the showers upon the grass.*

*-Deuteronomy 32:2*

## Rain

*I'm going to make them and everything that surrounds my hill a blessing.*

*I'll send down the rain! At the appropriate time, there will be a rainstorm of blessing!*

*-Ezekiel 34:26, ISV*

# INTRODUCTION

Are you currently experiencing a drought season in your life?

A season that feels like nothing is living, yet nothing is birthing.

A season where you feel exhausted from running and you've never reached the finish line.

A season of stagnation, despair, and your ears seem dull to the voice of God.

My Sibling in Christ (S.I.C.), you are not alone!

Unfortunately, this is a season when many believers lose hope. The reason being, they do not know the purpose of this season, or how to survive it. Without knowledge, there will be a daily battle against the ***Three-D's, disappointment, discouragement, and dismay.***

During my season of drought, I felt as if I was looking for an exit out of a maze. I was discouraged and ready to throw in the towel, up until God gave me a revelation. A powerful revelatory insight that taught me the purpose of a drought and how to survive it.

*S.I.C., please do not get weary in this season. Scripture states in Galatians 6:9,*

***"And let us not be weary in well doing; for in due season, we shall reap if we faint not."***

*The New Living Translation says,* ***"So let's not get tired of doing what is good. At just the right time we will reap a harvest of blessings if we don't give up."***

*Let's begin*, as you may know, the seasons must change, because every season has a purpose; both naturally and spiritually. *Ecclesiastes 3 states, "there is a season and time for everything."*

Through study, I compared spiritual seasons and their purpose to the four natural seasons, Spring (*new beginnings*), Summer (*labor*), Fall (*harvest*), and Winter (*drought*). The correlation between a natural winter season and a spiritual drought season is identical.

During a drought, nothing blooms, and in the winter nothing blooms; however, both have a significant purpose.

Winter is a season of timing, shifting, resting, reflection, ceased growth, appreciation, intimacy, and cleansing. In the winter, days are short, nights are longer, and studies have shown that this season can bring on major depression or anxiety. Most of our time is spent indoors which allows more intimacy with those we love; and for others, loneliness.

In the winter, it does not look like the flowers or tree buds are going to bloom, but beneath the surface, the seeds are germinating. Winter is also a time of preparation and expectancy for the arrival of spring.

The comparison: While in a drought season, we often feel depressed, anxious, and alone. Days are faint, long nights are weary, and it seems like all growth has ceased. My S.I.C., this is a season to trust in God's timing, rest in His Presence, reflect on His Word, appreciate His Goodness, and cleanse yourself through consecration (you cannot shift with old baggage). God desires intimacy and oneness with you during this season.

This may sound insane, but a drought season is also a time of preparation and expectation. This is certainly a season to prepare yourself for what God is about to do with a great expectation!

In a natural drought, the soil looks dry and cracked, but once it rains, new sprouts begin to spring forth. My S.I.C., every fruitful seed that you have planted is birthing beneath the surface and new growth is springing forth!

*"Behold, I will do a new thing; now it shall spring forth; shall ye not know it? I will even make a way in the wilderness, and rivers in the desert." -Isaiah 43:19, KJV*

*"For I am about to do something new. See, I have already begun! Do you not see it? I will make a pathway through the wilderness. I will create rivers in the dry wasteland." -NLT*

Isaiah 43:19 is a "Praise Break" scripture, I get fired up every time I read it!

***God is up to something and He is doing it mightily in your life!***

*I got excited for a moment, but let's continue!* A drought is a necessary season, as it prepares you for the new. Old things must fade away to make room for the brand-new.

In the winter, you know without a doubt that the

cold-bitter season will soon pass, and spring will be arriving. You must have the same faith in God to believe without a doubt that this old season will pass, and your new season is approaching soon.

*Snippet*

*The revelation I received was profound. First, I had believed that I am the daughter of an Almighty King and nothing less. Furthermore, I needed to accept the authority I was given in order to boldly walk in my calling.*

*Secondly, As I prayed, God showed me a vision of fire coming from my mouth like a dragon. The fire symbolized the power in strategic prayers. Strategic prayers are target prayers, they are like an arrow in the center of a bull's eye.*

*Lastly, God helped me to understand that a drought season is required for humility and growth.*

*The drought season has definitely taught me patience. I have learned to patiently wait on God, trust in His timing, and stand firmly on His Word.*

*Yes, I know a dry season can be tough. However, a drought is not meant to break you: rather, it is meant to make you. It will increase your strength, wisdom, and faith. This season will compel you to stand strong when everything around you is falling.*

*"Humble yourselves therefore under the mighty hand of God,*

*that He may exalt you in due time."*

*-1 Peter 5:6*

Are you ready for the shifting? Elijah was a prophet of God; whose prayers shifted an atmosphere from drought to rain. S.I.C., I need you to allow this to marinate in your spirit. The key word is prayer. An atmosphere cannot be shifted without the power of strategic prayers, combined with authority, boldness, and faith.

*So, he went to Zarephath. As he arrived at the gates of the village, he saw a widow gathering sticks, and he asked her, "Would you please bring me a little water in a cup?"*

*As she was going to get it, he called to her, "Bring me a bite of bread, too.*

*But she said, "I swear by the Lord your God that I don't have a single piece of bread in the house. And I have only a handful of flour left in the jar and a little cooking oil in the bottom of the jug. I was just gathering a few sticks to cook this last meal, and then my son and I will die."*

*But Elijah said to her, "Don't be afraid!" Go ahead and do just what you've said but make a little bread for me first. Then use what's left to prepare a meal for yourself and your son.*

*For this is what the Lord, the God of Israel, says: There will always be flour and olive oil left in your containers until the time when the Lord sends rain and the crops grow again!"*

*So, she did as Elijah said, and she and Elijah and her family continued to eat for many days.*

*There was always enough flour and olive oil left in the containers, just as the Lord had promised through Elijah. -1 Kings 17: 9-16, NLT*

*Side-note: The three key words that stood out in this text are "Don't be afraid!" In the KJV it says, "Fear not!". Fear is a blocker to any blessing. Fear will hinder the Word of God, because it will cause a person to doubt (**Your faith has made you whole. Luke 17:19**). Elijah perceived that the widow was fearful about sharing her last meal; so, he encouraged her not to be afraid. The spirit of fear oftentimes will hinder a believer from acting on God's Word. Fear produces stagnation, and it will delay what God told you to do, write a book, start a business, ministry, etc. We are not only meant to be titled as Believers, but we must be total believers in all aspects of our lives, and not doubters.*

The widow woman and her son were preparing to die during the drought, but because we have an Amazing God, He sent Elijah. The widow woman believed the prophetic words spoken through Elijah. She blessed Elijah with the little she had, and in return, she was blessed with an overflow.

You see, the widow's atmosphere was changed, not the season. It was still a drought; nonetheless, God supplied her with what she needed to survive. Her atmosphere was shifted from not enough, to more than enough in a season when everything had dried up.

Yes, a prophetic word can bless you tremendously during a drought season! Our God is the same God who spoke through Elijah and blessed the widow woman.

## Do you believe He can do the same today?

Yes, prophets have been graced with a greater level of prophetic authority; however, every child of God has been given power and authority by the Holy Spirit (Acts 1:8). We all have been authorized to shift, decree, declare, speak to dry bones, call forth the rain, and to speak things that are not, as though they were!

While in the drought, God dropped strategic prophetic prayers in my spirit like rain. Powerful prayers that shifted the drought atmosphere. I pray these prayers will cause an overflow and bless you abundantly as they have truly blessed me.

*Get ready! It's time to shift the atmosphere!*

## *Instructions*

- *Each prayer must be accompanied by faith. Prayer without faith is a dead and useless prayer, its destination is the ceiling. Our prayers are meant to shift atmospheres and reach heaven, and not drop to the floor!*

- *Pray each prayer with confidence and boldness. We cannot shift an atmosphere praying like a baby or fearfully.*

- *Journal your progress, revelations, insight, etc. during the next 21 days in your Prophetic Rain Journal.*

- *Pray, preferably in the early morning, because it will help shift the atmosphere and set the tone for the rest of the day.*

- *Fast during the 21 days (abstain from foods). Fasting is a prayer booster!*

- *Fasting will also help break any strongholds, barriers, or excess baggage.*

- *A basic 12 am -12 noon fast is suggested for individuals who are new to fasting or are taking medications.*

**"Is not this the fast that I have chosen? to loose the bands of wickedness,**

**to undo the heavy burdens,**

**and to let the oppressed go free, and that ye break every yoke?"**

**-Isaiah 58:6**

*Please seek the advice of a healthcare professional before fasting, especially if you have a medical condition.*

*If you have any questions regarding the instructions, the prayers, or testimonies; please send all emails to bytammyj@gmail.com*

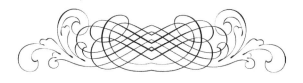

*"Elias was a man subject to like passions as we are, and he prayed earnestly that it might not rain:*

*and it rained not on the earth by the space of three years and six months. And he prayed again, and the heaven gave rain, and the earth brought forth her fruit."*

**-James 5:17**

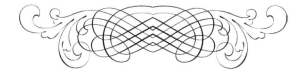

## I RELEASE

*Do you not know that you are God's temple and that God's Spirit dwells in you? -1 Corinthians 3:16, ESV*

*I* release complaining and I replace it with a praise! *1 Thessalonians 5:18 says, "In everything give thanks; for this is the will of God in Christ Jesus concerning me."*

I release worry and I replace it with a steadfast mind according to Your Word in *Isaiah 26:3, "You will keep in perfect peace those whose minds are steadfast, because they trust in You."*

I release fear and I replace it with Your Word in *2 Timothy 1:7, "God has not given me the spirit of fear but of power, and of love, and of a sound mind! Yea, though I walk through the valley of the shadow of death, I will fear no evil because You, Oh Lord are with me!"*

I release doubt and I replace it with a Now Faith! *Hebrew 11:1 says, "Now faith is the substance of things hoped for, the evidence of things not seen."*

I release disappointment, discouragement, and despair, and I replace it with *Philippians 4:7, "The peace of God which passes all understanding, shall keep my heart and mind through Christ Jesus."*

I am released from every stronghold and all areas of bondage. Today, I replace it with Your Mighty Hand according to Your Word in ***Exodus 6:6, "and I will redeem you with a stretched-out arm."***

In the Mighty Name of Jesus, I pray. Amen!

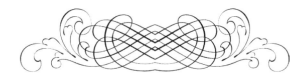

*"Be glad then, ye children of Zion, and rejoice in the Lord your God:*

*for he hath given you the former rain moderately, and he will cause to come down for you the rain,*

*the former rain, and the latter rain in the first month."*

**-Joel 2:23**

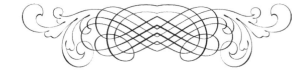

## 2nd Day

# BIND AND LOOSE

*"Truly I tell you, whatever you bind on earth will be bound in heaven, and whatever you loose on earth will be loosed in heaven." -Matthew 18:18, NIV*

*I* come in the authority and the Name of Jesus Christ to bind and loose!

I bind every negative confession I've spoken over my own life and I loose Proverbs 16:24, "Pleasant words are as a honeycomb, sweet to the taste and health to my body."

I bind every negative thought and I loose 2 Corinthians 10:5, "I Cast down imaginations and every high thing that exalted itself against the knowledge of God and bringing into captivity every thought to the obedience of Christ."

Today, I choose to change my thought pattern according to my Father's Word in Philippians 4:8, "Whatsoever things are true, whatsoever things honest, whatsoever things are just, whatsoever things are pure, whatsoever things are lovely, whatsoever things are of good report; if there be any virtue, and if there be any praise, think on these things!"

I bind every word curse and incantation that was spoken against my life and I loose Isaiah 54:17, "No weapon formed against me shall prosper, and every tongue which rises against me in judgment You shall condemn."

In the name of Jesus, I bind every fiery dart that is launched against me, and I loose the hedge of protection in Job 1:10, "Have you not placed a hedge on every side around me, my house, and everything I have."

I bind every demonic accuser that is sent to destroy my character with false accusations. Every wicked scheme shall stop, fall, and crumble at my feet. In Jesus' Name!

I bind all blocking spirits, eavesdropper spirits, demonic interferences, demonic influence, demonic attachments, demonic plans, and demonic assassinations sent to kill my purpose and destiny, and I loose Jeremiah 29:11, "For I know the thoughts that I think towards you, said the Lord, thoughts of peace and not of evil, to give me an expected end."

In Jesus' Name. Amen!

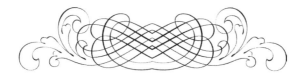

*"Drop down, ye heavens, from above,*

*and let the skies pour down righteousness:*

*let the earth open, and let them bring forth salvation, and let righteousness*

*spring up together; I the LORD have created it."*

**-Isaiah 45:8**

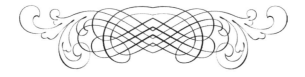

## 3rd Day

# I AM FREE!

*"If the Son sets you free, you will be free indeed."*
*-John 8:36*

I am free from a vagabond mindset!
I am free from double-mindedness!
I am free from an Egyptian mindset!
I am free from a wilderness mindset!
I am free from all infirmities!
I am free from depression!
I am free from oppression!
I am free from heartache!
I am free from unforgiveness!
I am free from procrastination!
I am free from stagnation!
I am free from weariness!
I am free from heaviness!
I am free from brokenness!
I am free from false burdens!
I am free from ungodly relationships!
I am free from ungodly thoughts!
I am free!
In Jesus' Name, Amen!

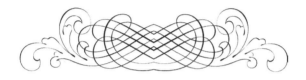

*"Then I will give you rain in due season,*
*and the land shall yield her increase,*
*and the trees of the field shall yield their fruit."*
*-Leviticus 26:4*

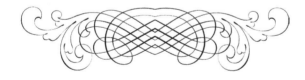

## 4th Day

# BREAKING UP FALLOW GROUND

*"Sow to yourselves in righteousness, reap in mercy; break up your fallow ground: for it is time to seek the LORD, till He come and rain righteousness upon you."*

*-Hosea 10:12*

### A Word from The Lord

*I* come as a Gardner to prepare your heart for the harvest. I cannot, nor will not plant or rain on fallow ground. I come to gather the thorns in your heart, pluck the unrighteous weeds that have grown, and to dislodge any stubborn rocks.

I come to place your heart in the Refining Fire to burn off everything that is not pleasing to Me.

I am preparing your spirit.

I am preparing your heart.

I am preparing you for miracles.

I am preparing you for signs and wonders.

I am preparing you for my blessings

I am preparing you for the RAIN!

said, The LORD.

*Father, I thank You, because Your spoken Word will not return to You void, but It will do exactly what You sent It to accomplish. And it is so!*

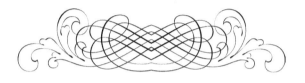

*"For I will pour water upon him that is thirsty,*

*and floods upon the dry ground: I will pour my spirit upon thy seed,*

*and my blessing upon thine offspring."*

*-Isaiah 44:3*

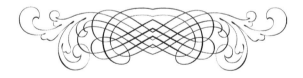

## 5th Day

## SPIRITUAL ALIGNMENT

*"You shall also decree a thing, and it shall be established for you: and the light shall shine upon you always."*

*-Job 22:28 NASB*

### Prophetic Declaration

Today, I decree and declare physical healing, mental healing, and spiritual healing for myself and those connected to me. I come in alignment with *Isaiah 53:5, My Father's Word says, He was wounded for my transgressions, He was bruised for my iniquities: the chastisement of my peace was upon him, and with his stripes, I AM HEALED!*

I decree and declare my thoughts come in alignment with Colossians *3:2, For Your Word says, think on things above and not beneath!*

I decree and declare my feet walk in alignment with *Psalm 32:23, The steps of a good man are ordered.*

I decree and declare I come in alignment with divine open doors according to *Deuteronomy 28:6, My Father says, I am blessed when I come in and blessed when I go out!*

I decree and declare all my needs come in alignment with *Philippians 4:19, For my God, will supply all my needs according to His riches in Glory through Christ Jesus!*

I decree and declare every lack in my life come in alignment with *Psalm 34:10. Father You said, I will lack no good thing!*

My finances have been on the wrong side of the road, going in the wrong direction. They have been going left, but today I decree and declare my finances go right. I align my mind, creative ideas, and my bank account with Your Promise in *Deuteronomy 8:18,*

Your Word says, *For it is He that giveth me power to get wealth, that He may establish his covenant...*

*"The blessing of the LORD, it maketh rich, and he addeth no sorrow with it." -Proverbs 10:22*

Father, Your Word also says in *Galatians 3:28, that if I belong to You, then I am Abrahams's seed, heirs according to the promise.* Father, Your Word also says in, *Psalm 35:27 that You have pleasure in the prosperity of Your servant.*

I decree and declare I am a lender according to Your Word in *Deuteronomy 15:6 that says, I will lend and not borrow!*

I decree and declare the holes in my pockets are stitched up, because I have considered Your Ways!

I decree and declare *Deuteronomy 28:13 over my life, I am the head and not the tail, I am above and not beneath*!

Opportunities have been passing me by, it seems like everyone is being blessed, except me. Today, I decree and declare the plans of God in *Jeremiah 29:11 will overrule in my life and grant me the promise of an expected end!*

I decree and declare the seeds I have planted shall spring up and produce a bountiful blessing, according to *2 Corinthians 9:6, "But this I say, he which soweth sparingly shall reap also sparingly; and he which soweth bountifully shall reap also bountifully."*

I decree and declare victory belongs to me according to *1 Corinthians 15:57. My Father has given me the victory through Our Lord Jesus Christ!*

Today I am shifting the drought atmosphere!

In Jesus' Name, Amen!

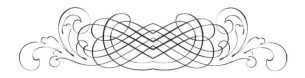

*"Then shall we know, if we follow*
*on to know the LORD: his going forth is prepared as*
*the morning;*
*and he shall come unto us as the rain,*
*as the latter and former rain unto the earth."*
*-Hosea 6:3*

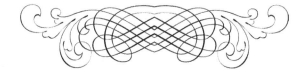

## 6th Day

## YOU CALLED ME!

*"I will give you the treasures of darkness and hidden wealth of secret places, so that you may know that it is I, the God of Israel, who call you by your name."*
*-Isaiah 45:3*

### A Word from the Lord

I have called you by your name.

I strategically, fearfully, and wonderfully created you.

I have ordered your steps and lightened your path.

You are the apple of My eye and the sheep of My pasture.

Delight in Me and I will give you the fullness thereof.

Turn not with weeping and sorrow, yet sing and rejoice.

For I have heard your cries and I am swift to respond.

Seek not your way or own understanding but firmly stand on My Word.

Be assured that I have never left you, nor will I ever leave.

Allow My Voice to lead you through every dark place and My arms to carry you through the deep waters. You are my child and I have called you by your name.

Said, The Lord

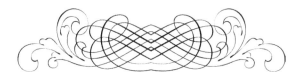

*"As the rain and the snow come down from heaven, and do not return to it without watering the earth and making it bud and flourish so that it yields seed for the sower and bread for the eater,"*

*- Isaiah 55:10, NIV*

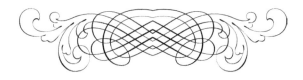

# 7th Day

## CALL ON MY NAME

***"I will offer you a sacrifice of thanksgiving and call on the Name of the Lord." Psalms 116:17 -NLT***

𝒥call upon Your Name, ABBA. I call You Father, I call You Daddy. I call You Omni-Present, Omni-Scient, and Omni-Potent, A Name that is above all names. A Name that the heavens and earth must obey! There is POWER in Your GREAT Name!

You are, El Eloah, My God Who is Strong and Mighty!

Elohim, My God, Who is the Creator of all!

El Shaddai, The Almighty One!

I worship You, Adonai, because You are Lord!

You are Jehovah, The Great I Am!

Jehovah Jireh, My God Who Provides!

Jehovah Rapha, My God Who Heals!

Jehovah Nissi, The Lord is my Banner and I raise You up High on today!

Jehovah M'Kaddesh, My Lord Who Sanctifies!

Jehovah Shalom. You Are my Peace in the time of turmoil!

Jehovah Elohim, You Are The Lords of Lords and beside You, there is no other!

Jehovah Tsidkenu, My Lord of Righteousness!

Oh, How Excellent is Your Name!

Jehovah Shammah, My God that is Always There!

Jehovah Sabaoth, You are the Lord of Host!

El Elyon, You Are the Most High God!

El Roi, My God that sees all!

El Olam, From Everlasting to Everlasting, You are my God!

El Gibhor, You Are a Mighty Warrior, and nothing is too hard for You! Who is this King of Glory? The LORD strong and mighty, the Lord mighty in battle.

Jehovah Rohi, The Lord is my Shepard and I shall not want.

He makes me to lie down in green pastures. He leads me beside the still waters.

He restores my soul. He leads me in the paths of righteousness for His name's sake.

Yea, though I walk through the valley of the shadow of death,

I will fear no evil: for You *are* with me; thy rod and thy staff they comfort me.

You prepare a table before me in the presence of mine enemies:

You anoint my head with oil; my cup runs over.

Surely, goodness and mercy shall follow me all the days of my life:

and I will dwell in the house of the LORD forever!

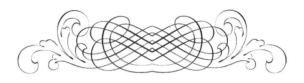

*"Neither say they in their heart, Let us now fear the LORD our God,*

*that giveth rain, both the former and the latter, in his season:*

*he reserveth unto us the appointed weeks of the harvest."*

*-Jeremiah 5:24*

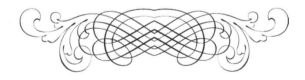

# 8ᵗʰ Day

## WHOSE REPORT WILL YOU BELIEVE?

***"Who hath believed our report? and to whom is the arm of the*** Lord ***revealed?" – Isaiah 53:1***

Whose report will I believe? Father, I believe your report is the truth.

I believe every Word you have said about me, and not what the enemy says.

I believe Your word will not return back to You void.

I believe my circumstances are changing!

I believe my season is shifting!

I believe nothing shall be impossible!

I believe You has given me the strength to do all things!

I believe Your Grace is sufficient!

I believed Your Mercy is renewed daily!

I believe all things will work together for my good!

I believe whatever I ask, it shall be given!

I believe You will never leave or forsake me!

I believe You sit up high and look down low!

I believe Heaven is Your throne and earth is Your footstool!

I believe the blind shall see, the deaf will hear, and the lame will walk!

I believe dry bones will come to life!

I believe Your Promises are Yes, and Amen!

*"Nevertheless, he left not himself without witness,
in that he did good, and gave us rain from heaven,
and fruitful seasons, filling our hearts
with food and gladness."*

*-Acts 14:17*

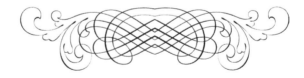

# REMEMBER

*"Remember the former things of old: for I am God, and there is none else; I am God, and there is none like me." -Isaiah 46:9*

### A Word from the Lord

Remember, it is I who held your hand and walked you through the darkest hours.

Remember, it is I who has captured every teardrop.

Remember, it is I who felt your deepest pain.

Remember, it is I who held back the high winds that tried to take you down.

Remember, it is I who caught you before you stumbled and fell.

When faced with the many challenges of life; remember, it is I who caused My Peace to prevail.

Remember, it is I who had the final answers to every question.

Remember, it is I who continues to uphold you with My Righteous right hand.

Remember, It Is I Who Still Is, And Forever Will Be.

Said, the Lord.

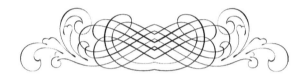

*"Who giveth rain upon the earth,*
*and sendeth waters upon the fields:"*
*-Job 5:10*

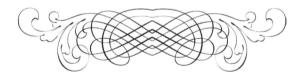

# A DAY OF REFLECTION

***This is the day which the Lord hath made; we will rejoice and be glad in it.***

***-Psalm 118:24***

Congratulations, you are stepping out of the old and into the new!

This is a day of reflection. A perfect day to reflect on the goodness of God.

As you may know, the number *10* signifies completeness in divine order. It also refers to a completed course. The ending of an old cycle and the beginning of something new.

I'm sure this 10th day is much different than the day you first started. By now, you should be able to feel a portion of the shifting. If you don't, that's okay, because you certainly will. Your faith, boldness, and the strategic prayers are going to shift the atmosphere in your life.

Have you been journaling? I encourage you to continue writing. Journaling is also a time to reflect on yourself. Today, as you reflect on God I also want you to reflect on the goodness inside of you.

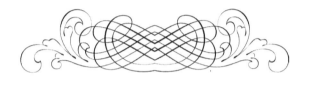

*"Then said the LORD unto Moses, Behold, I will* rain *bread from heaven for you; and the people shall go out and gather a certain rate every day, that I may prove them…"*

*-Exodus 16:4*

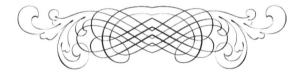

## 11th Day

## GOD OF ZION

**"I am the Lord the God of all mankind. Is anything too hard for me?"**

**-Jeremiah 32:27**

$\mathcal{M}$y God of Zion, nothing is too hard for you! Lord, I'm asking You to change the things within me that I don't have the power to change myself. Renew a right spirit in me! Father, You did it in the days of old and I ask that You do the same for me.

Create within me a great leader like David!

Grant me spiritual strength like Samson.

Bless me with wisdom like Solomon.

Cover me with favor like Esther.

Trust me with prosperity like Job.

I grab hold of the horns of the altar! I grab hold of the horns of the altar!

Like Jacob, I won't let go! I won't let go until you bless me!

Increase my substance, bless my first fruit, and bind the mouths of the cankerworm, locust, caterpillar, and the palmerworm that is continually trying to eat up my inheritance.

Right now, I'm standing firmly on Your promise in Joel 2:25, I will restore to you the years that the locust hath eaten, the cankerworm, and the caterpillar, and

the palmerworm…
Let the POWER in Your Mighty hands be released in my
life!
In Jesus' Name I ask, Amen!

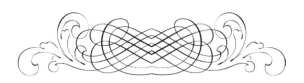

*"Do any of the worthless idols of the nations bring rain? Do the skies themselves send down showers? No, it is you, LORD our God. Therefore, our hope is in you, for you are the one who does all this."*

*-Jeremiah 14:22, NIV*

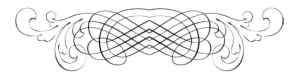

## POWER WORDS

*"Death and life are in the power of the tongue: and they that love it shall eat the fruit thereof."*

*-Proverbs 18:21*

*"The tongue has the power of life and death, and those who love it will eat its fruit." - NIV*

*H*eavenly Father, forgive me for not always being careful of my choice of words. Blessings and curses should not come out of the same mouth. Today, I call back and destroy; in the name of Jesus, every corruptible seed I have planted by speaking life-threatening words.

You have given me the power to speak death or life, and from this day forward I choose to speak *life.*

I choose to plant seeds that will produce good fruit and bring grace to the ears of those who listen.

I choose to speak words of *life* into my own life.

I choose to speak *life* into others.

I choose to speak *life* into every lifeless and dry situation.

I choose to bless and not curse.

I choose to build up and not tear down with my words.

I choose to plant and not uproot.

Father, I choose to speak words of hope, peace, strength, love, and encouragement.

Today, I choose to speak words that will bring you honor, praise, and glory.
In Jesus' Name, I pray. Amen

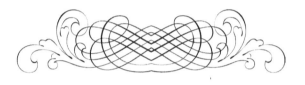

*"The LORD will send rain at the proper time from his rich treasury in the heavens and will bless all the work you do."*

*— Deuteronomy 28:12, NLT*

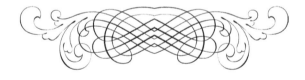

### *Note to the reader.*

Over the course of the next several days, you will see a change in the way the prayers are structured. There will be several blank spaces.

These blank spaces are provided for you to fill in the blanks to personalize the prayer. After you fill in the blanks, pray the prayer with power and boldness!

## JERICHO WALLS

*On the seventh day, the Israelites got up at dawn and marched around the town as they had done before. But this time, they went around the town seven times.*

*The seventh time around, as the priests sounded the long blast on their horns, Joshua commanded the people, "Shout! For the Lord has given you the town." -verse 15*

*When the people heard the sound of the rams' horns, they shouted as loud as they could. Suddenly, the walls of Jericho collapsed, and the Israelites charged straight into the town and captured it. - verse 20*

*-Joshua 6:15, 20, NLT*

Father, I thank You that a powerful "Shout!" knocked down the walls of Jericho. Today I "Shout!" down the Jericho walls in my life and I take full possession of the treasury!

I shout down every wall surrounding my heart, that I have built!

I shout down the walls blocking my blessings!

I shout down the walls to my _____!

I shout down the walls surrounding_____!

I shout down the walls that are separating_____!

I shout down the walls _____!

I shout down the walls preventing me from_____!
I shout down the walls _____!
I shout down the walls _____!
In the name of Jesus', I command every wall to come down!

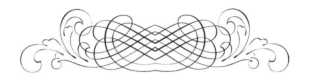

*"God, You poured out abundant rain on your inheritance.*
*When Israel was weary, you sustained her."*

**-Psalm 68:9, ISV**

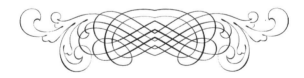

## DRY PLACE

*The hand of the LORD was upon me, and he brought me out in the Spirit of the LORD and set me down in the middle of the valley: it was full of bones.*

*And he led me around among them, and behold, there were very many on the surface of the valley, and behold, they were very dry.*

*And he said to me, "Son of man, can these bones live?" And I answered, "O Lord GOD, you know."*

*Then he said to me, "Prophesy over these bones and say to them, O dry bones, hear the word of the LORD.*

*Thus, says the Lord GOD to these bones: Behold, I will cause breath to enter you, and you shall live. – Ezekiel 37 1-5, ESV*

Today, I activate the prophetic voice inside of me! I take full authority over my

God-given rights. By the authority of Jesus Christ, I speak life to every dry place and I command you to breathe according to *Ezekiel 37*!

I call forth abundant life to the dry places, rain to the drought, and sun to the storm!

I cauterize the roots of every anti-Christ spirit that tries to steal, hinder, or deactivate my prophetic voice! I will not back down, I will not be quiet, I will stand firm, and I will prophesy, In the name of Jesus'

Right now, I speak life into every dry place that needs rain!

I speak life into_____my finances_____!

I speak life into_____!

I speak life into_____!

I speak life to_____!

In the name of Jesus, you shall live and not die!

I speak life to_____!

I speak life to _____!

I speak life to_____!

And it is so! In Jesus Name, Amen!

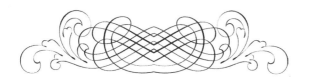

*"For the earth which drink in the rain that cometh oft upon it, and bringeth forth herbs meet for them by whom it is dressed, receive blessings from God."*

*-Hebrews 6:7*

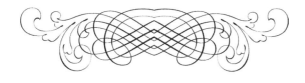

## FAVOR

*"Surely, LORD, you bless the righteous; you surround them with your favor as with a shield."*
*-Psalm 5:12, NIV*

Father, I thank You for the unmerited favor that covers me like a shield.

I thank You for favor, not because of something spectacular I did, but because of who You Are.

I thank You for favor <u>in my home!</u>

I thank You for favor in_____!

I thank You for favor_____!

Thank You, for favor_____!

Thank You for favor_____!

Thank You for favor with_____!

Thank You for blessing me with favor in my_____!

Thank You for unfailing favor!

Thank you for unseen favor!

Thank You for favor with You and people!

Thank You because Your anger is for a moment, but Your favor is for life!

Thank you for unbreakable favor!

In Jesus' Name, Amen!

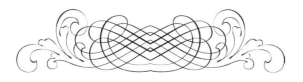

*"He covers the heavens with clouds, provides rain for the earth,*

*and makes the grass grow in mountain pastures."*

*– Psalm 147:8*

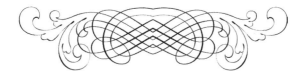

# PRAY FOR OTHERS

*"And the* Lord *turned the captivity of Job, when he prayed for his friends: also, the Lord gave Job twice as much as he had before." -Job 42:10*

*I* truly believe in praying for others. First, it is clearly the will of God and it pleases Him for us to pray for each other. Secondly, I love praying for God's people, and I enjoy seeing people set free from heavy burdens.

As Believers, we cannot get so consumed in our own issues that we forget to pray for others. The above scripture shows us the results of praying. Job's life changed dramatically when he stopped focusing on his situation and prayed for his friends. Romans 8:34 states, Jesus is sitting on the right hand of God, interceding on our behalf, and we must do the same. Somewhere, a person is going through exactly what you just came out of, or worse. So, I encourage you to put down your issues on today and pick up another's and intercede on their behalf like Job did.

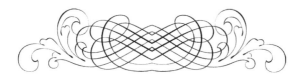

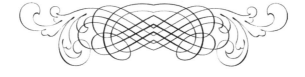

*"I will send rain for your land at the right time. I will send the autumn rain and the spring rain.*

*Then you can gather your grain, your new wine, and your oil."*

*– Deuteronomy 11-14, ERV*

## BREAKTHROUGH SEASON

*"God will stand up and break through in their presence. Then they will pass through the gate, going out by it. Their king will pass in front of themwith the LORD at their head."*

*-Micah 2:13, NLT*

### *Prophetic Declaration*

Lord, I thank You for Peace, Endurance, Stability, Favor, Increase, and Prosperity!

Today, I decree and declare restitution for everything that was lost, stolen, or withheld, In the Name of Jesus'!

I decree and declare strongholds are loosed, obstacles are removed, roadblocks are demolished, chains are broken, and straps are cut off. So, I may freely walk into my appointed breakthrough season. In the Name of Jesus'!

I decree and declare that everything in my life that has been held in bondage, is now set free, In Jesus' Name!

I decree and declare my Breakthrough gate wide open!

I come in the authority of Jesus Christ, bombarding the entryway to my Breakthrough, and slaying every giant blocking my entrance with the same stone David used to slay Goliath.

Today, I am A Champion, I am a Warrior, I am Victorious, and

I am an Overcomer!

Father, I gently embrace my Turnaround season! I thank You in advance for overflow, open doors, open windows, divine connections, and divine appointments!

I thank You for the one "YES!" that overrules the many "NO's!"

Thank You, because many others will be blessed, due to my Breakthrough! Today, I receive the Anointing of Fresh Oil and New Rain to gracefully walk into my Breakthrough Season; in Jesus' Miraculous Name I pray, Amen!

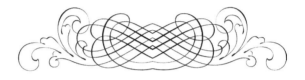

*"He directs the snow to fall on the earth and tells the rain to pour down."*

*–Job 37:6, NLT*

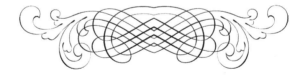

## DAY OF WORSHIP

*Those who blew the trumpets and those who sang were like one person. They made one sound when they praised and thanked the Lord. They made a loud noise with the trumpets, cymbals, and instruments of music. They praised the Lord, singing, "The Lord is good. His faithful love will last forever."*

*Then the Lord's Temple was filled with a cloud.*

*The priests could not continue to serve because of the cloud, because the Glory of the Lord filled the Temple.*

*- 2 Chronicles 5:13-14, ERV*

Heaven is waiting for your response!

Being in the presence of God's Glory is such a wonderful experience. No one should ever be the same afterward; it's an encounter like none other.

Allow me to share some knowledge with you. God responds to worship, and not complaints. You are not waiting on God, but God is waiting on YOU!

God is waiting on a certain response, your praise.

Scripture states, God inhabits the praises of His people, which means He will come and dwell among us during our worship to Him. Your worship calls God into your atmosphere, and when He enters, everything must shift.

Let's briefly examine David, 1 Samuel 16:23 states, that whenever a tormenting spirit troubled Saul, David would come and musically worship with his instrument and the spirit would go away. David was a prophet (Acts 2:30) and when he worshiped prophetically through his music, it shifted the atmosphere.

*S.I.C.* I need you to understand *that prophetic worship, prophetic prayers, and prophetic declarations* can shift any atmosphere. Now, you may be saying, "I'm not a prophet." Well, allow me to tell you what the scriptures read in Joel 2:28, God said He will pour out His spirit on all flesh and your sons and daughters will prophesy.

*Sidebar: Before I go any further, I want to make sure we are on the same page with prophecy. I am not stating that every believer walks in the office of a prophet. However, if you are a Holy Spirit filled believer; you are authorized to prophetically speak over your life.*

*You can prophesy and speak things that are not, into how you would like them to be, according to the will of God. You are basically speaking your future into your present.*

**Then Jesus said to the disciples, "Have faith in God. I tell you the truth, you can say to this mountain, 'May you be lifted up and thrown into the sea,' and it will happen.**
**But you must really believe it will happen and have no doubt in your heart. I tell you, you can pray for anything, and if you believe that you've received it, it will be yours.**
**–Mark 11:22-24, NLT**

*We having the same spirit of faith, according as it is written, I believed, and therefore have I spoken; we also believe, and therefore speak. -2 Corinthians 4:13*

This level of prophetic authority will work in your life, but not necessarily in the lives of others.

The authority to frequently speak into another's personal life is given to a believer who walks in the office of a prophet. They have been given the grace to be the mouthpiece of God.

The Prophetic office carries a greater level of authority, and you must be called by God (Jeremiah 1:5), trained, (1 Samuel 19:18-20), and ordained (Acts 14:23) to fluently and accurately speak into the lives of others.

*Let us come before his presence with thanksgiving and make a joyful noise unto him with psalms.*

*- Psalms 95:2*

Today, I need you to press into an intimate worship with Father. Get consumed in His Presence and saturated in His Love.

Express to Abba how Marvelous He is, and what He means to you. Tell God how much you love and adore Him. S.I.C, don't hold back, release a high praise unto the Lord! A praise that will get heaven's attention. A sound that is going to shake and shift the atmosphere.

In the midst of your worship, I want you to prophesy over yourself. Begin to speak what God says about you, speak your words in a future tense and not a present tense. e.g., "I am healed!" instead of "I'm going to be healed."

In Genesis, the Bibles says the earth was without form, void, and dark and God said, "Let there be light!" There was light because God spoke the light into existence. He did not say it was going to be light; There is a significant difference between the two.

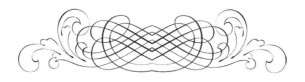

*"Ask the Lord for rain in the spring,*
*for he makes the storm clouds.*
*And he will send showers of rain*
*so every field becomes a lush pasture."*

*– Zechariah 10:1*

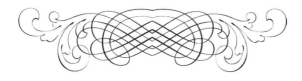

## THE SHIFT

*"And when the day of Pentecost was fully come, they were all with one accord in one place.*

*And suddenly there came a sound from heaven as of a rushing mighty wind, and it filled all the house where they were sitting." -Acts 2:1-2*

On the day of Pentecost, a mighty shift took place. A rushing wind that shifted the atmosphere and changed the lives of many generations to follow. Father, I thank You because that same sound of a mighty rushing wind resides within me. I am an atmosphere shifter!

Today, I shift the atmosphere by shifting my mentality.

Today, I shift the atmosphere by shifting the words I speak!

Today, I shift the atmosphere by shifting the company I keep.

Today, my surrounding must shift in order for my situation to shift.

Today, I shift my_____!

I shift the_____!

I shift_____!

I shift_____!

I shift_____!
I shift_____!
Father, I thank You for the authority to shift!
In Jesus' Name. And it is so!

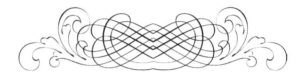

*"He shall come down like rain upon the mown grass;*
*as showers that water the earth."*
*-Psalms 72:6*

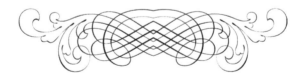

## 20th Day

## THE SOUND OF RAIN

*"And Elijah said unto Ahab, Get thee up, eat and drink; for there is a sound of abundance of rain."*

*-1 Kings 18:41*

Father God, I can hear the sound of abundant rain!
Daily, I will walk by faith and not by sight. Even though I
    cannot physically see the rain, I can spiritually hear it.
I hear the sound of overflow!
I hear the sound of victory!
I can hear the sound of heaven moving on my behalf!
I hear the sound of the floodgates opening!
I hear the sound of keys rattling and doors unlocking!
Father, I hear the sound of the atmosphere shifting!
Abba, I hear the sound!
The sound lets me know that my breakthrough is near!
The sound is alerting me to position myself for the release
    of Your Blessings!
Lord, I will rise up and rejoice at the sound of the rain!
I will stand up and dance to the sound of victory!
I will raise my voice in adoration!
Lord, I lift up clean hands to receive Your Abundant Rain!
In the Name of Jesus Christ. Amen!

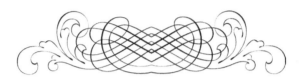

*And I will make them and the places round about my hill a blessing;*

*and I will cause the shower to come down in his season;*

*there shall be showers of blessing."*

*-Ezekiel 34:26*

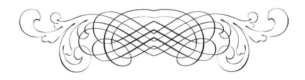

## PROPHETIC RAIN

*I* prophesy to you through the prophetic grace and authority that has been gifted to me.

I call forth the Prophetic Rain in your life. I prophesy the rain of God's blessings shall fall and overtake you!

I prophesy this is a season of a turnaround, a season of abundant favor, a season of victory, a season of more than enough, a season of expansion, and a season of heights.

I call forth the rain on your behalf. I speak to every dry place to be filled with the abundance of rain.

I speak to every fruitful seed that has been planted, I command it to come forth with a great harvest; in the Mighty Name of Jesus!

I speak overflow in your life, home, and resources!

I speak to every lifeless situation, and I command it to live. Right Now, In the Name of Jesus!

I speak to every wall, and I command it to fall; right now, in the Name of Jesus

Christ of Nazareth!

I command every closed door to be divinely opened, expeditiously!

I command every deaf and blinding spirit to enter a dry and waterless place, so you may clearly see your destiny and hear your purpose calling!

I speak Deuteronomy 45:8 over your life. The Lord shall command the blessing upon you in thy storehouses, and in all that you settest thine hand unto; and he shall bless thee in the land which the Lord thy God giveth thee.

Father, it is Your Will that those who are obedient to Your Word be blessed.

Father, I ask that You send forth the rain!

Rain God, Rain God, Rain God! Rain on them God and Reign in the lives of Your

People!

Father, allow new testimonies to burst forth and let the praises of Your Glory, Arise!

I prophesy that every word I have spoken will not fall to a dry ground.

Today, if you only believe it, you shall receive.

And it is so; In Jesus' Name. Amen!

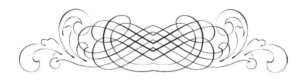

*"In the light of the king's countenance is life;
and his favor is as a cloud of the latter rain."*
*-Proverbs 16:15*

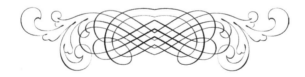

## *Abbreviations*

Prophet – nataph, (naw-taf) to pour down; gently fall, drip; to (drip words) preach, prophesy. -Hebrew, Strong Concordance

KJV, King James Version

ESV, English Standard Version

ISV, International Standard Version

NASB, New American Standard Bible

NIV, New International Version

NLT, New Living Translation

*OTHER BOOKS BY TAMMY JAE*
*10 Steps Closer to God*
*Behind the Mask*

*COMING SOON!*
*A Mother's Thorn*
*A Praying Woman*
*Get Out, Anxiety!*